IMMEDIATE KNOWLEDGE
AND HAPPINESS

By the same author

THE NATURE OF MAN ACCORDING TO THE VEDANTA
(Second Edition 1970. Routledge and Kegan Paul)

IMMEDIATE KNOWLEDGE AND HAPPINESS

(SADHYOMUKTI)

The Vedantic Doctrine of Non-Duality

by
JOHN LEVY
(PREMANANDANATH)

SENTIENT PUBLICATIONS, LLC
PO BOX 1851, BOULDER CO 80306, 303-443-2188
contact@sentientpublications.com
www.sentientpublications.com

First Sentient Publications Edition 2024

This work is in the public domain in the United States of America, and possibly other nations. Within the United States, you may freely copy and distribute this work, as no entity (individual or corporate) has a copyright on the body of the work.

Cover design by Stefan Prodanovic

Publishers Cataloging-in-Publication Data
Levy, John, 1910-1976
   Immediate knowledge and happiness : the vedantic doctrine of non-duality/
John Levy.~1st Sentient Publications ed.
p. cm
ISBN 978-1-59181-314-9
1. Vedanta. 2. Self (Philosophy) 3. Man (Hinduism) I. Title.
B132.V3L38 2024 128-dc22
2023952281

10 9 8 7 6 5 4 3 2 1

SENTIENT PUBLICATIONS
A Limited Liability Company
PO Box 1851
Boulder, CO 80306
www.sentientpublications.com

Contents

Philosophy and You	1
I. The Meaning of Man	1
II. Man, God, and the World	13
III. Mind and Consciousness	26
IV. Love, Happiness, and Guidance	38
V. The Present Eternity	50
VI. Freedom	64
The Universal Religion	73
Dedication	79
About this book...	81

Foreword

"Philosophy and You" is the title of a series of broadcast talks given by me in August and September 1946 over the Army Signals Station at Madras Area Headquarters as a part of the Forces' Educational Programme. I was then serving in the British Army and attached to the Army Educational Corps. It was at the invitation of the Madras Area Education Officer, Major Rajagopal Menon (now Colonel) that the talks were given. They were published, at the time, in the *Madras Area Broadcast Review* and now, with a few small changes and three new paragraphs and a conclusion, they are presented in book form. Much of the familiar style of the original is retained as being quite in tune with a statement of what is nearest the heart of every man.

>   SRI ATMANANDA GURU
>   is my Master whose name I
>   place with love and veneration
>   at the head of this work.

Philosophy and You

I. THE MEANING OF MAN

As an introduction to this series of talks entitled "Philosophy and You", let me begin by saying a few words about the title itself. Philosophy, which literally means the love of wisdom, is regarded almost universally as an art for art's sake and therefore as having no practical value. That this is usually the case, and in the West especially so, only shows that what generally passes for philosophy is often only idle speculation; and unfortunately, the impression thus created has naturally put off many people who would otherwise be anxious to reap the benefits of its study and practice. The truth is that of all human activities, this is certainly the most practical, being the only one which aims at giving and does really give final and satisfying results. Its purpose is to answer the questions that occur to every thinking man and woman, such questions as, "What am I?" "What is the purpose of this existence?" "What is life?" and "What happens after death?"

Many systems of philosophy claim to answer these questions, but not many can offer at the same time the means to experience directly the truths they contain;

and when the means are lacking, it is a sure sign that the answers themselves are inadequate. When the right answers are given *and* understood, they bring about such a revolution in the mind of the seeker that until he has experienced them in the most concrete manner, he feels he cannot rest.

Now the system of philosophy upon which I am basing these talks is that known as Vedanta, because I find that it maintains a perfect balance of theory and practice and is therefore capable of immediate application. It is known also as Advaita or Non-Duality, and has been practised in India from the most ancient times right up to the present. The title of these talks might have been "Hindu Philosophy" but this would certainly have given a false impression. We are not at all concerned with what Hindus, Greeks or Chinamen, Hebrews, Christians, or Muslims as such think: we are concerned only with finding answers to our questions. The meaning of Vedanta, the name of this system, is the end or attainment of knowledge. We can talk of this or that religion, but we cannot talk of this or that philosophy, although I know well that people do, and those especially who like to compare things; but that is all on the surface. This is not going to be an appreciation of Hindu philosophy, but an attempt to find a solution to those problems which have always faced mankind. So without any further delay, and in the most simple and direct manner, let us begin our search. What is man?

We have to begin with man because it is as men that we ask these questions. It is therefore in connection with ourselves that these problems arise; we must know also whence they come. The first one was "What am I?"; the others were "What is the purpose of this existence?" "What is life?" and "What happens after death?" It will be seen that if the first question, "What am I?" is answered to our satisfaction, the others will also stand explained. Now what we have to understand is the nature of the being who refers to himself as "I". We may say, for example, "I am hungry", "I feel cold", "I sat down", "I am going to-morrow", or "May I speak with you?"; in all these examples, the same "I" is given different roles. It is the body that is hungry, the body that feels cold, the body that sat, the body that will go to-morrow and the body which is to do the speaking. We are, in fact, identifying ourselves here with our bodies. We also identify ourselves with our minds. If we say, for instance, "I think", "I remember", "I wish", "I can imagine" or "I wonder", does it not show it clearly, for it is the mind that thinks and remembers and desires and imagines things and asks questions. And what does the question "What am I" show? It shows beyond doubt that a man is something more than just a mind and a body; otherwise, why should such a question be asked? It is obvious to all that man possesses these two things. He can never be satisfied by being told that he is nothing more than that. And yet, although it is obvious, we all seem to spend our lives as though we thought quite the opposite. What I mean is this: I said just now that we obviously possess a body and a mind. But with most of us, a case of simple possession is mistaken for identity with the thing possessed: this is wrong. I shall prove that this identification of ourselves with our minds and bodies is mistaken.

Anyone can see that a man's body is always changing. There is the infant's body, the child's and the adolescent's; it then comes to maturity and passing through middle age, it declines into old age and then it dies. But the identity of the owner of the body does not change; it is the same person right the way through. And the same changeless identity is seen to be behind the mind which also changes constantly, passing through the same states from infancy to old age and death. It can easily be seen from this that our real self, what we refer to as "I" when we speak of ourselves, has no solid connection with our bodies and minds: it gets connected only when we wrongly attribute actions of the body and mind to the real self. Instead of saying, "I am hungry" or "I think", would it not be proper to say, "My body is hungry" or "My mind thinks"? Please don't imagine that I'm suggesting we should all start talking in this manner; but we should most certainly *think* it, because such thought would help us to end the false association of what changes with the changeless within us, for false this association undoubtedly is. How can such different things be partners? For instance, at the time we say "I heard a sound" or "I had an idea", the body that heard the sound or the mind which had the idea are no longer exactly what they were: they have both changed. What remains constant is the entity we refer to as "I". By superimposing the idea of body and mind on this changeless entity, we wrongly give it the attribute of changeability.

Something that is changing cannot by itself observe the change in something else, because in order to observe change, some permanence in the seer is needed. Now it is the real self we refer to as "I" which observes the changes in the body and the mind. So this again proves that we are at bottom changeless. And this is also the principle of memory. If there were not some changeless background upon which thoughts and preceptions left their mark, how could they be recalled after their occurrence? Extending this to the future, we see people making plans and expressing hopes. This shows that there is within us a principle which covers both the future and the past and is therefore beyond the passage of time. It affords still further evidence that we are in ourselves above change, and therefore beyond body and mind.

Again, we can remember only those things that have been known or perceived by us. They would otherwise have made no impression on our memories. This applies alike to the material things we observe through the organs of sense, and the thoughts and feelings that rise in our minds. And this is not all: when we remember that we met a friend, it is not only his image that comes up, but also our own as it appeared at the time of the meeting. Or if we think of our having written a letter yesterday, we see also our body's writing it. Likewise, when we remember our previous thoughts and feelings, we remember as well the thinker who had them, that is to say, ourselves or rather our minds. But I said just now that we remember only those things we have known or perceived. If we remember our bodies and minds along with the things we observed and the thoughts we had, our bodies and minds must also have been witnessed by us in just the same way. It follows then that we are their witness and not the actual thinker, enjoyer, seer or doer. Thinking, enjoying, seeing and doing are functions peculiar to the mind and the body. So once again, we find ourselves to be beyond all change.

There is another kind of experience we all have and that is sleep. When we are having a dream, it all appears to be just as real as the world we see when we are awake. Who indeed could be sure that he isn't dreaming at this moment? This is by the way, and I shall return to it later. The point I want to make is this, that in a dream, we get another body: our waking body is lying on the bed. In dreamless sleep, we are conscious of neither the body nor the mind. When we wake up we say we enjoyed sound sleep. By sound sleep, we mean that we knew nothing and this nothing or no thing relates to the things we perceive when awake or dreaming. What is meant is that there were no thoughts; and in their absence, mind cannot be said to function. But in spite of this, we were quite conscious, for if this were not so, we could not say we enjoyed sound sleep. And that we do enjoy ourselves in that state is proved both by the annoyance we feel if someone disturbs it and by the anguish of sleeplessness. From this also it is clear that we are quite separate from the mind and, at the same time, our real nature is one of consciousness, since it subsists when all else is gone.

I shall give one more proof that our essential being is something other than the mind and the body we claim to possess. When I say I own a house I don't imply that I am a house. On the contrary, I cannot possibly be one. The sense of possessing a house is in no way different from the sense of possessing a mind or a body. A body, like a house, is an object, and so is a mind. But I am the possessor of the object and therefore not the object itself, in this case the body or the mind. In other words, if I possess a body and a mind, I am clearly other than the body or the mind.

After having seen in all these ways what we are not, we are now in a position to see what we really are: we have already seen in connection with sleep that we are in ourselves pure consciousness. Our relation to space is through our bodies. But we are not the body. We are therefore beyond the limitations of space, and so infinite. And our relation to time is through our minds, which are made up of a succession of thoughts and feelings. But we are not the mind. We are therefore beyond the limitations of time, and so eternal. We are infinite and eternal and of the nature of absolute consciousness. This is not a play upon words. It is the truth, and if we think otherwise, it is only the mind that thinks so. But we are beyond the mind, and thoughts cannot reach us. We set out to seek an answer to the question, "What am I", and to find where this question comes from. There is no doubt that the question comes from the depths of our being, from our innermost self, from the changeless entity we call "I"; and the understanding we have gained also comes from there. It cannot come from the mind, although it appears as a thought, because the answer takes us beyond it: whereas a question that is purely mental, such as a mathematical problem, leads to an answer on the same level.

And what of the other questions? They are related to life and death and the purpose of it all. To speak first of death, every body knows that physical death occurs when the life principle passes out of the body, which then ceases to function. Life is defined by the dictionary as the active principle peculiar to animals and plants and common to them all, while an animal is described as an organized being endowed with life, sensation, and voluntary motion. Now, if life is common to all living things, it cannot be something individual even though we do speak of animal or plant life, your life or my life. If it is not individual, what is it? Surely it must be something universal, and we call universal life existence. And it is clear that the birth or death of an individual has no effect upon existence. It will continue to be just what it was. But at the same time, an individual obviously has a part in existence through what we call life, without which the other two qualities of sensation and voluntary motion could not subsist. If we examine these, we find that sensation is a function of the body. Sensations are the impressions the body conveys to the mind through the sense-organs, and voluntary motion is imposed upon the body by thought, that is to say, by the mind. We are back again where we started with life instead of the changeless principle we call "I", but since life is itself another name for existence which we found to be changeless and is common to all individuals, the I-principle and existence are one. So we may say that pure existence is known as life when it becomes limited or individualized by association with a body and a mind. There is of course, a contradiction in this statement, and I expect that it will have been noticed: the infinite can never become limited as stated here. But so long as we are considering life as it appears, we are unable to avoid making such contradictions. The same thing is present in what I said about the false association of the real self with the body and mind. We have to proceed by steps, and I shall return to the question in another talk when I discuss the problem of how an infinite and eternal reality assumes or seems to assume the limitations of time and space.

Now this apparent digression is not really one at all. It gives us the clue we want in order to answer the question about the purpose of this existence. Well, however surprising it may sound, I say it has none. There is no real purpose in this so-called earthly existence, because earthly existence as such is unreal. Or I may say that the purpose of existence, if purpose it is, is to exist. You may already be able to grasp this, but in any case, I have no doubt that it will soon become evident to those who are patient and curious enough to attend to my subsequent talks. Meanwhile, we can say that the purpose of this existence has been fulfilled for those men who ask themselves questions of the kind we are now considering and whose sincerity and earnestness lead them to find the only true answer. They then become identified with their true self instead of with a false and limited one, and are no longer liable to birth and death, which are attributes of the body. I do not propose to discuss the theory of re-incarnation, or birth and re-birth; but there is no doubt that the only satisfactory explanation of the difference in human development, talent, circumstances, and general tendencies between one man and another, visible to all, is this: that previous lives have made them so. If this is accepted, then what happens after death is patent. Unless the man who dies knows *and feels* that he is, in his self, quite distinct and separate from his body and mind, he will be born again and again until he comes to realize that lasting happiness is to be found where it alone exists, that is, beyond the everchanging circumstances of life.

People spend all their lives seeking happiness in one way or another, and the proof that they never really obtain it is that they never stop seeking it. Or when they do think they have found it, they cling to whatever it is they believe to be the cause, lest they lose it. Whereas the happiness we seek is beyond all circumstance. I remember once being asked why I was so preoccupied with philosophy. I replied that I sought a happiness that nothing could spoil, and my questioner then said his ideal would be realized as soon as he could marry the lady of his choice. I was cruel enough to ask him what would happen if the lady died. He had no answer.

Now there is the possibility of my being misunderstood on account of what I have just said. Some people think it would be necessary to renounce all worldly pleasures and activities and take to an ascetic life in order to attain perfection. But this is not at all what I mean. Knowing full well that we are not one with our bodies or minds through which we have our connection with the world, and knowing also that it is they who act, think, enjoy or suffer, we can safely leave it to them to work out their own possibilities, and ourselves remain unattached by an inward act. This again may be given an interpretation that is not mine. It is not a licence for people to do just what they like and go against accepted moral standards. Morality has as its purpose the control and reduction of egoism and it is not likely that a man who seeks the truth would do things that would increase his sense of individuality. I shall conclude my talk with a few words about this.

Egoism, or the sense of individuality, is nothing other than the wrong identification of the real self with the body and mind that has been the subject of this talk. When one man murders another in order to rob him of his money, it is only because he has allowed his body so to dominate his reason that for the time being, he has become a body. The same is true of similar other acts which we call bad or sinful. Acts are bad, wicked or sinful only when the body-idea is in the forefront. The very same acts, when done in another setting, can have precisely the opposite effect on the doer. Thus, to risk one's life in battle in order to defend one's people against aggression or to earn legitimate profit through honest labour cannot in any way be said to be the effects of egoism. Or if we consider the mental plane, argument employed for the establishment of some truth is fully justified, while a man who uses his wits simply to score victories over his rivals is associating himself with his mind, like learned men who pride themselves on their knowledge. To be charitable out of compassion is to give up so much of one's egoism: to give money in order to be praised is simply to increase it. Good and evil, or virtue and vice, can therefore be defined in the following manner: virtue is that which lessens the sense of individuality while vice is that which raises it.

So another age-old problem has been solved in a few words in the light of what we have previously come to see. But I feel myself obliged to add that virtue and vice and other moral qualities are characteristics of the mind and not of the real self. Although it is no doubt good to think of such things, too much attention should not be paid to them if the ultimate reality is the goal, otherwise, instead of paying attention to that, we shall be paying attention to the very thing from which we wish to separate ourselves. That is why I said that the body and the mind may very well be left to look after themselves, provided always, and I lay emphasis on the word always, provided that we always remember what is our real nature.

In the meantime it may be wondered why nothing has been said about God. Yes, but wasn't this an enquiry into the nature of man? However, now that we have come to know something about ourselves, we shall be in a better position to understand something about God, and I shall begin the next talk with God as my subject.

II. Man, God, and the World

These talks began with an enquiry into the nature of man. That was the proper way to start, because as I explained then, it is as men that we ask the fundamental questions we were considering, such questions as "What am I"? and "What is the purpose of this existence?" If we are to get a correct answer to a question, we must first of all know something of the person who puts it, otherwise we may find that we are talking at cross purposes: in this case, the question concerned ourselves, so there was a double reason for it.

We found that man appears at first sight to be a combination of the changeless principle we refer to as "I" with a body and a mind, both of which are always changing. As an example of this, we say, "I am a man". At times, we associate ourselves with the body when we say, "I am hungry" or "I am enjoying good health", and at times with the mind, when we say, "I think" or "I remember." But in spite of this identification of the "I", or real self, with the body and the mind, man remains at bottom changeless. Otherwise he couldn't remember what previously *was* in order to compare it with what now *is*, and thus know that a change has taken place. From this, we were able to see that a man is entirely distinct and separate from his mind and body; and we also saw that he can be without either of these as in deep sleep, and yet remain fully conscious. In deep sleep, although there are no thoughts, this absence of thought is clearly perceived by something else, for we say, "I enjoyed sound sleep" or "I slept so well that I knew nothing until I woke up". This was how I proved that in his real self, a man is not one with his body and mind but of the nature of consciousness, in which his thoughts and perceptions come and go.

This brief summary of what I said in the first talk has been necessary in order now to consider what is God. I closed it by saying that having come to know something of ourselves, we were in a position to understand something about God; and that I would begin my next talk with God as my subject.

God is defined by the dictionary as the supreme being and the ruler and creator of the universe. So the universe must first of all be examined. Of what does it consist? Let the dictionary again speak! It says under universe: "All existing things, the whole creation and the creator." Now, all things that are made up of matter occupy a certain amount of space. Air is also material. And a vacuum, which if it exists is devoid of matter, also takes up space. Thus we find that space is the background of matter; and while all material things are ceaselessly undergoing change, space itself is changeless, being simply the name we give to the invisible and indefinite something which contains and runs through the whole material universe. So we can say that while the universe is composed of individual bodies, amongst which the heavenly bodies and of course this earth are included, the universal body is nothing other than space. It is common to them all and yet not identical, because though the bodies are changing, space itself never changes.

If we take a broad view of the world, we can clearly see that everything happens according to a plan. The movements of the earth round the sun and the moon round the earth, as well as this planet's rotation on its own axis which together form our measure of time, day and night, and summer and winter, are certainly not accidental. From this, we can understand that there is a universal mind. I have given as an example of this the orderly movement of the earth and the moon, as it is apparent to all. If we examine the human or any other individual mind, we shall find the same thing. We all know the story of King Canute and the waves. His people thought he was divine, so he had his throne taken down to the seashore, and he commanded the tide not to come in. But it came in just the same, and he thereby showed them that there existed a mind greater than his own. The ebb and flow of the tide is brought about by the moon twice in a lunar day, in other words, it is subject to time. So is mind. We cannot say where a thought was but we can say when it occurred. Thoughts come one after another in succession and that means time. Time is therefore the changeless background of our minds. But time is something quite relative. We call a year about 365 days, whereas the planet Jupiter has a year of some 12 of ours. But time implies existence and existence is common to all the different measures of time. Existence is therefore universal and as such cannot be affected by the changes of time and space, which appear as its parts. I have said that time and space are both changeless, and now I speak of their changes. What I meant, of course, was that relative to individual matter, universal space is changeless, and relative to every particular series, so also is universal time. Space and time are taken here simply as names of ideas; in fact, space is known only by matter and time by thoughts. In this last sense, which is also the higher, space and time do change while existence, common to them both, is changeless.

Now, if we cast our minds back to what I said about the changeless principle we refer to as "I" in relation to man, we can understand that this changeless existence has precisely the same position in respect of the universe as a whole. Because we see ourselves as persons, we also ascribe personality to universal existence which then becomes the universal being. It is this universal being whom we call God. Compared to our own limited persons, and in terms of our own bodies and minds, he is infinite and eternal, almighty, all-knowing, and free, since he is not limited by space and time. And because it is impossible to imagine what other origin the universe with all its living beings can have had, he is also seen as the creator of all and we see ourselves as his creatures. This is what a man, who has not considered carefully what he is himself, thinks of God. But I have shown that we are also beyond the limitations of time and space, being quite independent of our minds and bodies. Can there be two infinities? Surely not. It is through our bodies that we have our connection with space and through our minds that we are connected with time. It is through our real self, what people vaguely call the soul, that we have our connection with the universal being called God. If we are bold enough to face it squarely, this leads us to the conclusion that God and man, when seen as they really are, that is to say apart from their universal and individual attributes, are one and the same. To make it clearer, we have only to consider water. Water appears as ocean, and the ocean throws up waves and foam. Now the waves and the foam are like individual worlds and beings, and the ocean is like the universe. But apart from the names we give to each different form, they are really nothing but water. The ocean is water, foam and waves are water. And so it is with man and God. If we wish to approach the truth, we can either make ourselves one with the universal being and thus get to the background of all, or we can dive deep within ourselves and find the ultimate truth there; this is more direct. It is the path followed by Vedantins and I shall have more to say about it later.

Meanwhile, there are several points in what I have been saying that need further explanation. One of these is the question of personality. There can be no difficulty in understanding that one person is distinguishable from another only by the differences between bodies and minds. When we consider man, not as he appears, but as the changeless principle beyond name and form that he really is, what is there by which any distinction between one and another can be made? Thus we are all one and at the same time, impersonal. In the case of God who is by definition incomparable, how can *he* be personal? He is only thought of as personal by those who cannot rise above their own personalities. They liken themselves to God or God to themselves when they say that God created man in his own image. But all who have followed what I have been saying can very well understand this position, and it again leads us to the conclusion that God and man are the same, because when both are impersonal, that is to say, having nothing upon which any marks of distinction can appear, how can they be distinguished? But make no mistake: it is not as God, the lord of the Universe, and man, the possessor of a body and a mind, that they are one. It is neither as God nor as man, but as that which is common to both. And for those who find it difficult not to think of the ultimate reality as a person, I have provided the best of arguments that God exists if there is a man. I have shown that corresponding to the changeless principle standing as witness to the individual mind and body, there is also a changeless principle standing as the witness to the universal body and mind. This is a truth that no poor agnostic or atheist can deny. As for ourselves, we are free to go beyond limitations because we know that in fact we are beyond all limitation. I think I have made it perfectly clear.

There is another point, and a very important one, that requires elucidation. Our dictionary spoke of God as the creator of the universe, and the universe as the whole creation and the creator taken together. Well, how *did* the universe come into being? This question is often put in connection with space, time and causality, or the chain of cause and effect. Everything we perceive in terms of time and space or mind and body is always the effect of some cause, and the cause in its turn is the effect of some other cause and so on. The universe as a whole is also seen to be an effect when considered as the work of a creator. If we enquire about the origin of the material universe, does it not really mean, "Where or in what place did space come into being"? If we ask the same question about the subtle universe or time, does it not mean, "When or at what moment did time begin?" And if we ask about the first cause, is it not the same as asking, "What is the cause of cause?" All these questions lead us nowhere, like the old problem of the chicken and the egg: which came first? The question about space by the word "Where" makes space the starting-point of space, as though space already existed; the second by the word "when" makes time begin in time, and the third merely turns cause into effect! All sorts of theories have been suggested as solutions to these absurd questions but obviously, the whole can never be explained in terms of its parts. Modern so-called science dances in agony around this sort of folly. The old thinkers with far greater penetration stated that no beginning could be posited, but that the universe comes to an end when it is properly understood. This is much nearer to the truth, and satisfies those who without analysing memory, take cause and effect for granted. I shall take this up in due course and shall now go into the question of time and space.

If we analyse space, we find it to be the interval between any particular points. It is impossible to think of any object without thinking of space. It is impossible also to think of space without some thought of size, and size is a property of matter. Space and matter are therefore inseparable. Now, to see an interval takes time, because it requires at least three thoughts: one of each extreme and one of the intervening space. So space is really nothing but time. We might say that space is the embodiment of time, but it would not be true, because we still have to think of it. In other words, space exists only when we think of it; and just as matter is inseparable from space, so is space itself inseparable from thought. And we have already seen that thought is inseparable from time. And what is time? We saw that space is the name we give to the invisible and indefinite something which contains and runs through the material universe. Is not time the name we give to the intangible and indefinite something in which our thoughts occur? We measure time by fixed periods or intervals which we think of as past, present or future. But the present is already past when we think of it and that is why I called time intangible. That which is always present is consciousness, whether we think of past or future. It is impossible to think of time without thinking of succession, nor can we think of succession without referring to time. But the actual thought appears *now* in consciousness, and that is eternal because it is ever present. Consciousness is present when there is thought and it is present when there is no thought. If not, how could we speak of there being no thought? We become aware of time when we think of it: if we don't think of it, we are not aware of it. But we never cease to be aware or conscious, for consciousness never sleeps. Thus thought and time are one, one in consciousness.

In reducing space into time and time into consciousness, or by connecting time with thought and space with matter, it has been taken for granted that time and space are integral parts of the universe. I am now going to examine them in a more direct manner. We saw that in relation to matter, space appears as its changeless background and relative to the succession of thoughts, time also appears as changeless. But as space is known only by matter and time by thoughts, time and space are simply names we give to ideas. Why do the ideas of space and time arise? They arise because we poor men cannot bear to think that all we cling to is transient, that our bodies die and our thoughts all vanish. So we try always to attach the changeless within us to whatever fleeting perceptions and passing pleasures our bodies and minds may have, lest we lose them; this we do by our claiming to be the doer and enjoyer in the name of the changeless I-myself. Similarly, we project a changeless background upon all the physical and subtle objects of our perception by the ideas of space and time, not knowing that it is we ourselves as awareness who are their sole permanent principle. We imagine a space to be the container of matter and a time to be the container of thoughts, whereas it is in consciousness which is their real container that all our perceptions come and go. But space and time are themselves only thoughts, and therefore they too are objects of perception, and far from being changeless, they change according to the state of their perceiver.

For instance, the measure both of time and of space differs in waking and dreaming while in deep sleep, there is none. We know what remains: it is consciousness and it is in consciousness that they arise, and thus space and time are nothing other than that, wrongly associated with our various perceptions and as such, they point directly to our real nature. If thought of in this light they will help us to become established there.

But creation has not been explained so far. I have gone the opposite way, and reduced the universe through space and time into consciousness. In the light of this, we shall now be able to understand how the world comes into being. I say purposely "comes" and not "came" into being. We shall also see why philosophers seek the truth within rather than without. To seek the truth outside oneself, one must become one with all. But this all exists only when we think of it. If the objection were to be raised that others may be thinking of it even if we are not, I would reply that it is we who think of those others, and if we don't think of them, they also don't exist. We found that in deep sleep, a man is without body and mind, because consciousness has, so to speak, withdrawn itself from them into itself. Without it, the mind cannot function, and without mind, there is no body. The objection may again be raised that others can see one's body lying inert upon the bed. The reply is the same: others exist when we think of them. There is absolutely no proof that they exist until our thoughts bring them into being. The old saying that seeing is believing is literally true. On waking up, we become aware of the outer world only when we become aware of our bodies. When the sense of body goes, the world goes with it. When thoughts subside, so does the sense of time. But consciousness remains. Therefore the universe rises and subsides in consciousness. It has no existence apart from ourselves. So if we must posit a creator, it is we who create it when we think of it. We destroy it when we cease thinking of it and consciousness remains. That is myself. Or yourself. Or simply self, for it is impersonal.

I have gone further than I intended to go at this stage, but I think it has been better to do so, for we have disposed of the outer world and seen that if we know ourselves, we shall know everything else, because nothing exists apart from ourselves. In my next talk, I shall show how this applies to our daily existence and transforms it into something quite beyond ordinary life.

In the meantime, I must make a last reference to God in relation to the universe. At the risk of offending those who may have found it difficult to follow or accept what has been said about the universe, I have to say the same thing about God. He exists when we think of him, and not otherwise. He is the creation of man. I refer to the idea of a personal God, not to the changeless background of the universe with which our own changeless background is one. If I put it in this way, it will become crystal clear: Every man's body had a beginning; that required two other bodies, each of which also required two bodies and so on, till the whole of mankind is involved. Bodies need food and clothing and implements to procure them, and that brings in the whole animal, vegetable and mineral kingdoms and the earth we inhabit. The earth itself cannot exist on its own, and this in its turn brings in the solar system and all the others until the whole universe is covered. And finally, the universe must have someone to regulate it and so we get God. From so small a beginning, that is to say, from a body and a mind, the rest of the world follows. But in looking at things like this, a man is standing aloof as an individual from all the rest, whereas in fact his body and mind are just a minute part of the whole. All this universe had to be brought into existence for the sole purpose of supporting one single life! But as soon as we recognize as our real nature the background of consciousness in which our minds and bodies come and go, we become free and make that our centre. We become detached from our bodies and minds as such and the whole world goes with them. Everything is then seen as consciousness itself. We are no longer men, so how can there be a universe or a God? They exist in thought only and not in reality. Reality stands above change; the absence of change is the standard of reality. In my next talk, I shall speak of man from this angle and show how even though we may be engaged in every kind of worldly activity, there is a means to remain centred in the changeless reality and this entails an analysis of life, thoughts and feelings of which a man is made.

    And to conclude this talk, I shall deal with a doubt that will certainly have arisen in the minds of many. It may be expressed as follows: "If our real self is beyond the mind and cannot, as I said in the first talk, be reached by thought, what use at all is there in talking about it?" Well, I say that everyone must ask himself this question because as long as it remains unanswered, it is likely to block the way to spiritual certainty. It is before this problem that agnostics bow their heads and turn their backs. Religion is impotent here also. If the truth is beyond the mind, how can we possibly know what it is? The answer is that the mind becomes one with whatever it has as its object. If the object is material, thought also becomes material and acts or perceives or enjoys through the body. If the object is mental, the thought of it may remain as thought and not go outwards through the body. If the truth or consciousness becomes the object of thought, thought merges into consciousness. As I said in the first talk, our understanding of these matters comes from our innermost self. I shall now prove it. I said just now that if we make what is beyond the mind the object of thought, thought merges into consciousness. This statement was to help understanding but it contains an error. Consciousness can never be the object of our thought, since it is in or by consciousness that our mind functions. We see the world by the light of the sun, we can see also its source, the sun, but never the light itself. Similarly, we can never look at consciousness. If the truth is to be understood, it can be understood by itself alone and that is why we are at liberty to think and talk about it, because by doing so, we silence the objections which the limited light of our minds raises and then in that stillness the truth that is within us shines by itself. Coming back to where we were, we wrongly claim *we* understood. The truth with its understanding is always present but we cover it up with our thoughts and feelings which are tainted by the idea that we are nothing but bodies and minds. When this wrong idea goes, spiritual certainty and lasting happiness are attained.

III. MIND AND CONSCIOUSNESS

In my last talk, I took up the problem of the universe, and by first reducing it into time and space, showed that in essence, it is nothing but consciousness. I showed that time and space correspond to mind and body through which we have our connection with it, and that it exists only when we become aware of our bodies and our minds. We become aware of the material world when we are conscious of our own bodies which are simply a part of it, and of time when we think of it, because thoughts appear in time; and time appears in consciousness which is there whether we are having thoughts or not. It is important to remember that although we talk of space, space is known in practice only through matter which we perceive through the physical organs of sense; the succession of time is known only through thought. This has the effect of making the world dependent upon our own bodies and minds, for we have no other means of establishing its existence. In short, time or the universal mind comes into being when we are mind-conscious; the material world or the universal body when we are body-conscious.

In the first talk, I proved that man is really something beyond the body and the mind, and so beyond time and space. In this talk, I am going to examine the body and mind from another angle, following on what was said in the last talk, of which I have just given a partial summary. This is called for by the remark I made to the effect that the world is dependent upon our bodies and minds. How then is the connection between ourselves and the world established? That is what I have now to show.

The body as such is dead matter; it has two essential functions. One is to act and the other to sense or perceive. Actions are done by the mouth, the arms, the legs, and the organs of reproduction and evacuation. Sense perceptions are gained through the five sense-organs, namely, the ears, the skin, the eyes, the tongue, and the nose, corresponding to sound, touch, sight, taste and smell. Without these, there could be no deliberate action, so it may be said that to gather impressions from without through the instruments of sense is the higher of the two functions. Because it is through the five sense-organs that the material world is known, the world itself is one of sound, touch, sight, taste and smell. To understand this, we have only to consider what a different world it would be if we had four instead of five organs of sense. For example, if none of us had the power to see, there would be no visible forms and we could only know a shape by its feel, without the help of visual imagination; fire could only be known by its heat and not by its light, and we could have very little idea of what goes on in the heavens. Or we may try to think what sort of world it would be if we had a sixth organ of sense. It would be very different. These two examples prove by themselves what I showed in my last talk, that the world is exactly what we make it. We make it when we hear, touch, see, taste or smell. We also make it when we think of it. And how do we think of it? We think of it always in terms of our senseorgans. We can, for instance, enjoy the thought of music; we hear it inwardly, and we can also think of things we have seen, such as the face of a friend or the house we live in and similarly we can summon up in our minds every other sensation.

It is evident from this that we not only have physical senseorgans, but also subtle or mental ones. We normally think in terms of our bodies; the mind works in the same way whether it comes out through the physical sense-organs or remains in the subtle ones. But the physical sense-organs work only when the mind is there. For example, if we are listening intently, we cannot feel a fly that has settled on our hand. If our mind wanders a little from our listening, and we become conscious of the fly, for that moment at least our attention is there and not in our hearing. In the same way, if we are walking along a street while immersed in thought, we hardly notice the things we pass. If we do happen to notice something in particular, our train of thought is automatically interrupted. What this signifies is that the mind can only be at one thing at a time. If it is in the sense of hearing, our ears alone function, if in the sense of touch, we can only feel, and if it is in none of the physical sense organs, as for instance, when we are thinking deeply or fast asleep, they cease to function altogether.

And just as the physical organs of sense need the presence of the mind to give them their mandate, so also does the mind require the presence of consciousness if it is to function. We are thinking and all of a sudden, there is a blank and it is only after an interval that we can think again. The same thing happens when we fall asleep. What does it mean? It means that consciousness has withdrawn from our mind and it is only when it returns that we can again have thoughts. In the first place, we saw that the sense-organs need the presence of mind to work; secondly that consciousness must be in the mind for thoughts to occur; we have already seen that mind can only be at one thing at a time, that is to say, there can only be one thought in consciousness or consciousness can only be in one thought at a time; and we may therefore conclude that without consciousness, neither the body nor the mind can function voluntarily. I say voluntarily, because it might be thought by some that the body *does* function on its own when we are asleep. But as a matter of fact, as I said in my last talk, when we are not aware of a thing, there is positively no proof that the thing exists; it is only when we think of it that it comes into being. If someone were to say that others can see our bodies when we are lying down asleep, I would answer that it is he who creates those others by thinking of them; so his argument falls away.

Now what is the practical application of this principle, the principle that without consciousness, neither the body nor the mind can work? In order to gain the fullest understanding from what I am going to say, it will be necessary to restate what we found the true nature of man to be. A man is conscious both when he is having thoughts and when he is without thought. Otherwise, it would not have been possible to say that one had been without it, because if consciousness were a part of the mind, if it were something merely mental, it would disappear with thought, and moreover, there could be no memory. But even when thought is absent, as in deep sleep or in the absent-mindedness I spoke of, consciousness does remain, for we know afterwards that we have been asleep or that we experienced a mental abeyance. In other words, beyond the body and the mind, there is a changeless principle we refer to as "I" and it is nothing other than this consciousness.

Having restated this fundamental truth, I shall now apply to everyday life and experience the conclusion we came to, namely that the knowledge we gain or the sensations we have of the outer world are due to the presence of consciousness in our minds and our sense-organs. I am obliged for the moment to use such an expression as "the presence of consciousness" because there are no others which can be used. If it is not correctly understood, it may easily lead to the wrong idea that when consciousness is absent, absent that is, from our bodies or minds, we are left without anything; whereas we are ourselves that consciousness and not bodies and minds, but we do not yet feel it to be so. Now, we have already seen how a man identifies his real self with his body when he says, for instance, "I hear a sound", meaning of course, "my ears hear a sound." Let us examine this carefully. When I say, "I hear a sound," two things are involved, the hearer of the sound and the sound that is heard. The sound is the object, the passive object of my perception, the thing perceived, and I am the subject, the active or conscious perceiver. I can only perceive a thing that is there to be perceived and the object can only be perceived when there is a perceiver to perceive it. Therefore, the perceiver and the perceived, or simply the subject and the object, are complementary. When we speak of a sound as being heard, we naturally assume there is someone to hear it. When we are awake or dreaming, we have countless sense perceptions. We hear, touch, see, taste or smell. That is how we have our contact with all the various things of the world. We can also perceive the same object through different organs of sense. For example, we can at once recognize an orange either by its appearance, its taste or its feel. And yet, although all manner of things are perceived through the five organs of sense, there is only one perceiver. It is always "I" who see or hear or feel, always the same "I". But we saw just now that the subject and the object are complements and inseparable. Can it be that the changeless "I", the real self, which is there whether there are perceptions or not, is inseparable from, let us say, the orange we are tasting? If so, we would be eating up our real self together with the orange! This is quite absurd, and the actual perceiver that is inseparable from the orange must be something other than ourself or the conscious principle. But we saw that the world is made up of sound, touch, sight, taste and smell, because it is through the corresponding organs alone that we are able to have our connection with it. So it is obviously the physical sense-organs and the material world that are inseparable, for the sense-organs are, in fact, an integral part of the material world.

How then does consciousness come in? Well, we have spoken so far only of the subject and the object, or the seer and the seen. These are bound together by their nature, and though I have taken as an example the case of material or gross perceptions, the same rule applies to subtle or mental perceptions or thoughts, to the thinker and the thing thought. Now there is a term which is common to the seer and the seen, or the thinker and the thing thought, and that is seeing or thinking. Perceiving is an experience that stands apart from the perceiver and the perceived. It is common to all perceptions, no matter what, and to all thoughts. It is indeed pure experience and I shall have more to say about it later. But what is now important is the fact that every experience is, if I may say so, a moment of pure consciousness. It is afterwards that we say "I thought of this or that" or "I saw a light". At the time of the actual experience, there was no such notion, there was consciousness alone. This is how consciousness comes in, and all we have to do to recognize it is to think[1] about it as often as possible. In due course, without our having to think of it specially, recognition will come up of its own accord, and then we stand established in pure consciousness.

There is another way of looking at the same thing. We saw that unless the mind is present in it, not one of the sense-organs can function. So instead of saying, as we did, just now, that the sense-organs and their objects are inseparable, we may say that the objects and the mind are. Now if the physical objects of perception and the mind which is subtle are inseparable, it means there is really no such thing as a physical object and the world is in fact purely mental. This is quite correct from the level of the mind, but is it all? No, for we also saw that mind itself functions only by the light of consciousness. Now clearly, what is inseparable from consciousness which is without name and form cannot be different in nature from it. Thus the world is nothing but consciousness. But how are we to experience it as such? Certainly, the plain thought of it will not bring about this realization, because we shall merely be bringing consciousness down to the mind-level, if that were possible. What we must do is to let every object of experience, including our body, be a pointer to consciousness, because it is necessarily present in every sensory experience.

The same thing must be done with regard to thoughts and feelings; they also bear witness to the presence of consciousness. By paying attention in this way to consciousness, our centre of gravity will gradually move from the superficial or the changing to the real or the changeless, and we shall thus become centred in our true nature. Normally, we seem to transfer our real centre to each object of perception. Our seeing an object we take as a proof of the object's existence and we place our interest there. We forget that both the seeing and the object proclaim the presence of consciousness, and that is far more important, indeed it's the only important thing, since it is the unity that runs through all this variety and enables us to know it as such. If we like to think of the world as real, it is because consciousness has made it so: it is in fact nothing but consciousness. Or we may say that it is unreal, because it vanishes when consciousness is not there, so the world as such cannot be real. Consciousness alone is real, since it is constant and never changes. There is nothing beside itself which *can* in any case change it. We give it names and forms, we call it man or mountain, but we know now that our perception of a man or a mountain points to this one thing, and so do our bodies and our minds: therefore, I say, let everything point to it; that is the way to realize it, that is to say, oneself.

I had promised in my last talk to explain how an infinite and eternal principle came to think of itself as being limited by time and space, and this is the right moment to do so. But there is no explanation, because the question itself is absurd, like the questions about time, space and causality. These questions seek an answer about the whole in terms of its parts, or its apparent parts, and this question ascribes doership to consciousness, which never acts, being changeless.[1] So let this, and all other questions of a similar nature, be allowed to point to consciousness without which they cannot arise. And it will come in time to be seen that this itself is the correct answer.

Now one of the things I set out to do in this talk was to consider man as made up of life, thoughts and feelings, in order to show how even though we may be engaged in worldly activities, we have a means to remain centred in our real self, and I have done it so far as thoughts are concerned. I showed how every thought and perception points to consciousness and that when properly viewed, thought *is* consciousness. I have already spoken of life in an earlier talk when I was relating individual life to universal existence. Life is pure existence wrongly thought of as limited by time and space or mind and body. This can be better understood now after all I have said since then, and to complete the picture, I have only to say this: that we stand above what appears as individual existence and it can be further proved in several ways. For example, a man will willingly allow a limb to be amputated if necessary; he knows full well that he will lose a part of his body but not a part of his life; again, for the sake of a cause he loves more than his life, he is prepared to risk his body in battle and this shows that consciously or unconsciously, he knows he is above life. When a man thus dissociates himself from his person, he betakes himself to something higher. Even a sportsman continually takes risks for the sake of enjoyment. We call it playing with death; death is simply a matter of leaving the body. Would one who really felt that death was final, risk it? And we see the same sort of thing with regard to the mind. So as to avoid suffering, people allow their brains to be paralysed for the time being by anaesthetics and drugs, knowing that they will not cease to exist thereby. They also lie down to sleep; that means they deliberately give up the mind. And if life becomes unbearable and they see no other escape, people commit suicide. Where do they wish to escape to? Into some happier state, evidently. Even if a man thinks he will cease to exist, it is he who thinks it; in other words, he stands beyond life and death, however unconsciously.

As for the emotional side of man, that part of him which feels love and hate, desire, pleasure and pain and passion, I propose to take it up in the next talk. The examples I have just now given in respect of life will help us. Moreover, the consideration of emotion will serve as background to a subject which has not so far been mentioned, one that is most essential. I refer to the guidance that everyone who wishes to advance in his progress towards the truth must have. This guidance is only to be had from one who knows what he says. We cannot approach the truth on our own, precisely because we think we are alone, that is to say, individuals. Someone is needed, therefore, who, having himself realized the truth, can impart it to others, and that is a thing that no mere learned man or book can ever do. It is sufficient for the moment that I have mentioned it and I shall return to it at the proper time.

Meanwhile, I shall now go on to a brief analysis of the working of the mind and so conclude this talk. Mind functions in four ways, and these are to gather impressions from without, to prefer one thing to another, to co-ordinate the different thoughts and exercise reason and choice, and finally to claim thought and action of the individual in the name of "I myself", what we may call the I-thought. I have already shown that there cannot be more than one thought at a time, and these four functions, for all their difference, are nevertheless thoughts only.

An examination of the I-thought will yield much fruit. At the time of doing, thinking or enjoying, there is no thought of being the doer, thinker or enjoyer. We are absorbed in the act, and it is only afterwards that we say, "I am doing or thinking or enjoying." When we are saying or thinking this, we are no longer the doer, thinker or enjoyer, because, as I said before, the mind can only be at one thing at a time. Now the thing we call "I" is really the impersonal self; it is also pure consciousness, and we individualize it because we think we are endowed with a body and a mind. But the fact that everything is claimed by this individual "I" bears witness to the presence of consciousness in whatever we connect it with, for it is this consciousness that runs through all our experiences. So all we have to do to get to consciousness, as we know already, is to disclaim the acts of the body and the mind instead of claiming them, and we shall thus become centred in our true nature. Obviously, in ordinary life, we are obliged to refer to ourselves as "I". But knowing now that the "I" is only a thought amongst others, we can either let it point to consciousness, or we can inwardly correct the false association of our real self with the body and mind. When either or both of these methods are diligently practised, we shall gradually become freed from our false attachment to body and mind and thus go beyond all circumstance and find perfect peace.

IV. Love, Happiness, and Guidance

In the previous talk, I spoke of man as being made up of life, thoughts, and feelings, and showed that life is the individual aspect of absolute existence while thoughts may be described as consciousness limited by time; but we have already seen that no such limitation is really possible. The same thing is true of absolute existence: how can it be confined to individual life? There is no explanation of such apparent limitations because as I have said, the whole cannot be explained in terms of its part. But we saw that the practical cause of this mistaken identification of the real and the unreal is the I-thought, that function of the mind which claims personal responsibility for the acts of the mind and the body. At the time of thinking, doing, perceiving or enjoying, there is no idea in the thinker, doer, perceiver or enjoyer that he is acting. It is only afterwards that he lays claim to what was in fact done by his body and mind. And as the act of claiming is itself a function of the mind, one thought amongst others, it has only to be recognized clearly as such for the wrong identification to cease. This was the conclusion we came to and I shall come to it again when I analyse memory. What I have now to examine is the nature of the third component part of man, that is to say, his feelings.

Our feelings, no matter what their nature, express our innate desire for happiness. Although I speak of our desire for happiness, the truth is that happiness abides within us always; but, since we seek it outside ourselves, it gets covered up by our associating it with various circumstances or objects. I proved that the truth and its understanding are ever-present in the core of our being; it is the same thing with happiness. Let us consider the case of desire. Suppose that the object of our desire is a house we wish to own. So long as we have not got possession of it, our mind is continually agitated with thoughts about its acquisition and what we intend to do with it afterwards. When we do at last possess it, our anxiety ceases and we experience happiness. What does this mean? It means that while the mind is active, there is no peace, that is to say, no peace of mind. When the mind comes to rest upon the object we desire, we find peace. Now when the mind is at rest, there can be no thought of the object. So it is not the object that gives us happiness but the absence of thought. We may say that happiness is obtained through objects, but it is not inherent in objects. If it were, then one object would suffice for a lifetime, whereas at one moment we are unhappy because we feel hunger or thirst, at another because some plan has failed to materialize, we feel miserable owing to illness, or we suffer from heat or cold and so on. Moreover, something that gave us pleasure as a child no longer satisfies us as we grow older, and what delights one man is repugnant to another, or the same thing alternatively pleases and displeases us. And in no case is the feeling of happiness complete; it invariably fades and leaves us dissatisfied.

All this shows that happiness is not to be found in objects. This has further proof in the fact that we enjoy sleeping. We saw in a previous talk how we remember our enjoyment of sound sleep. This example was taken to show that when mind is at rest, consciousness remains over. It also shows that peace and happiness remain with it. From this it can easily be understood that consciousness and happiness or peace are one and the same thing. Beyond the mind, there are no distinctions. We call the changeless background of man, consciousness in relation to his mind, and peace or happiness in relation to his heart or his feelings. And we know already that existence is the name we give to this changeless principle in relation to life. They are all one, and properly speaking, beyond all relativity.

To return now to the example of the house we wish to own, we all think that the object of our desire is the house. But is it really so? It is not; because once our desire is satisfied, we become desireless. Desire is an abstract something that in itself has nothing to do with objects. It is, so to speak, a conscious need or craving. We need fresh air to fill our lungs, and so long as air is freely available, we breathe it without the least feeling of desire. But if we enter a stuffy room, we become conscious of the lack of fresh air and we then begin to desire it; in other words, our mind becomes disturbed. As soon as the windows are opened, we feel a moment of relief, our mind comes to rest with the enjoyment of fresh air, and we think no more about it. So what we really desire is desirelessness, and not this or that object. Desirelessness is the state where there are no thoughts. Material objects are required by the body and subtle ones, such as answers to questions or the knowledge of facts, by the mind; but, as I have already made clear, we are not the body or the mind, but the changeless principle which we personify as I-myself. It is therefore an error to say, for instance, "I want a glass of water," when it is the body that wants it, and an error also to say, "I wish I knew the name of that man", or "I was glad to find a solution to the problem", when such things pertain to the mind and not to ourselves. We can now understand why most people believe that renunciation of the world is a necessary condition for the attainment of wisdom: they still associate their real being with their bodies and minds. They see that our connection with the world is maintained and strengthened by our desires, but they don't see that the real self has no desires at all, nor has it any aversions. Desire and aversion, or like and dislike, are the exclusive property of the mind; so why should we claim them? Once more, we see what a burden this I-thought is. Apart from its lending personality to the impersonal being that we really are, it gives substance to happiness and peace in the form of objects and circumstances.

This creates in its turn the vicious circle of desire and aversion, because if we once begin to identify happiness or unhappiness with some object, we seek or avoid that and similar objects again and again. However, it is now evident, I am sure, that all we have to do to escape from the hold of this vicious circle, which is the cause of birth and re-birth, is not to renounce desire but to disclaim enjoyment. This leads to the correct position, while renunciation is only the reverse side of the coin whose obverse side is longing. Desire, aversion and renunciation all refer to some sort of preference, and that gets us nowhere. The intelligent method to adopt, as I have just said, is to take the counter-thought after every feeling of enjoyment or displeasure that it concerns the mind and not myself, who am beyond the body and the mind. With a little practice it becomes automatic and, in time, the mistaken identification will end. We shall then find true felicity.

And what is love? It will help our understanding if we think of it in terms of give and take: love is seen to be either all-giving, all-taking, or an equal proportion of giving and taking; this is of course a broad view of it, and we need not go into all the variations of those three stages. Now love is something between two individuals. When it is all a question of taking, there is no consideration of the other person, and it is entirely selfish. When the giving and taking are in equal proportions, love is then mental and friendship is what we call it. It is, so to speak, a mutual contract where something in return is expected. Coming down to the physical plane, it is no longer entirely selfish, because the other person is also considered. And when it becomes a matter of giving alone, this is pure, selfless love. Nothing is expected in return and there is a complete identification of one's self with the other person. Happiness is derived here from one's being enjoyed by the other: that is, indeed, what always gives us the greatest pleasure. This desire to be enjoyed by others is often perverted by people's seeking popularity; it is spoilt only by this, that they want to get something back and that is of course selfish. But when the highest state of selfless love is reached, although it is manifested to others on the physical and mental planes, these become transformed.

When two people have risen to a level where each one can be entirely concerned with the other's happiness, perfect union is attained, because each is aware of one only and the enjoyment of each one is wholly dependent upon the other's enjoyment. Whether it is in connection with the body or the mind, it is the same. We have already seen that happiness has nothing to do with anything objective; it is the absolute state. When we pay attention to another's happiness, we lose the sense of our own body and mind and thus give up so much of our own egoism. A state will be reached where the idea of the other also subsides; this is when the idea of one's self as an individual goes, since obviously, the idea of there being others always presupposes the separate existence of one's self. Love, therefore, takes one to the ultimate reality in precisely the same manner as reason or knowledge. When all is seen as one in consciousness, the need of knowledge has gone, just as when all is one in love, there is no need to try to perfect one's relationship with others, because one is beyond all relationship.

The path of knowledge that has been the subject of previous talks is really one with the path of love. Philosophy, as I explained right at the beginning, means the love of wisdom. We seek the reality out of love; we desire to know the truth, in other words, it is the truth we love. There is a difference in the earlier stages, however, because although it is possible to attain the reality through love alone, people of an enquiring nature are liable to have doubts, and therefore higher reason has to be brought in to remove them. By higher reason, I refer to the inward-turning of the mind, as distinct from the heart. The path of knowledge is more especially suited to those we call, intellectual, but if we look at it objectively, it is evident that there can be no happiness in ignorance and no real knowledge without deep peace. Both knowledge and happiness exist; and therefore what in man appears as life, thoughts, and feelings, is at bottom absolute existence or being, absolute knowledge or awareness, and absolute bliss or love. These three names stand for the nameless reality, of which we now know something.

In the meantime, what I have said about love is not yet complete. I said that love is experienced between two persons, and that it appears on two planes, the physical and the mental. Pure love is beyond the body and the mind. What is it which we most love? We like this object or that because it gives us pleasure or happiness. But we saw that happiness stands apart from the objects through which we derive it. It is our real nature, so it is not the object, but our self that we love most, for that is what we are always seeking. As an example of pure love as it appears on the mental plane, we may take the case of a friend who is absent. We still think of him in separation with love, and even after his death. Similarly, a husband will have his wife's dead body buried or cremated without a pang. Do not these two examples show that true friendship is neither mental or physical, for when it reaches this level, it is beyond limitation and so is pure selfless love? Though nothing is expected in return, we still think of our dead friend with love. Now what is it that continues even after his death? Is it not the consciousness, without which we could not have known him before and think of him now? And what is this consciousness but our real self? So we see again that what we most love is ourselves, or rather the self, and not a body and a mind. I say *the* self because it is neither his nor ours. Pure love is, therefore, self-love, just as consciousness is self-knowledge or awareness; and existence, subsisting by itself, is pure being. In the last talk, in connection with life and existence, I gave the instance of a man who is prepared to sacrifice his body for some cause he loves more than his life. By transferring his love from his body and mind to some ideal with which he has identified himself, he proclaims that it is his self that he loves most.

I said just now that we can attain the truth through the path of love. This, however, must not be misinterpreted, as it so often is, as meaning that we have deliberately to extend our love to all men. I said also that when all is one in love, there is no need to try to perfect our relationship with others. This is a method that many attempt, but it is incapable of leading very far, because the very fact that we see others shows that we see ourselves as separate individuals, and nothing should be done which tends to keep up that illusion. Apart from this, even if we were to make a start at loving the whole of creation in order to become one with all, dozens of lives would hardly suffice to accomplish it. Mankind is by no means all, so that not only the present generation of men would have to be embraced but all previous generations and all those yet to come, along with the whole animal, vegetable and mineral kingdoms, not only here but in every other world in the universe, gross or subtle, including those which have long since ceased to exist and those which have still to come into being. In short, this path is entirely vain. If we wish to become one with all, we have only to identify ourselves with that consciousness without which nothing can exist. This is the one of the many, and having realized that, we become one with all, though strictly speaking, there is neither one nor many but only that consciousness.

Nevertheless it is possible to attain the truth through love and I shall explain how. In my last talk, I made a passing reference to the guidance needed by one who wishes to approach the truth. Philosophy, as we know, is the love of wisdom. But how can a man who thinks he is a body and a mind love what appears to him as an abstract something? He cannot, and so the truth must appear to him in the form of a man, one whom he feels to have known the truth, and who can speak to him in a familiar tongue and understand his temperament, and remove his doubts and difficulties, and take him beyond limitation by showing him out of his own experience what his real nature is. On the level of religion such a being appears as a descent of God upon earth in the form of a man. But we can now understand that such a thing is really quite impossible; everything must be examined and nothing taken for granted. No object, be it God himself, a prophet, a man, or a table can exist unless we perceive it. In other words, the truth cannot by any means be posited outside one's self. Besides, those extraordinary beings who have been taken by ordinary men to be God himself, or prophets, or sons of God, are remembered chiefly by what they taught their followers. Now the truth is eternal and doesn't change, but the manner of expressing it most certainly does, according to time and place, and the inner obstacles towards its understanding also, since each man and each generation of men differs in some respect from every other. If we are to depend upon teachings given hundreds or thousands of years ago, teachings given to people quite unlike ourselves in background, mental make-up and general temperament, we shall never obtain satisfaction. Moreover, the disciples of these ancient teachers had the essential advantage of a living presence and were not allowed to get away with their own interpretations as they do at present. Should we not also have the living presence of a sage to help us? We should and we can: there has always been an unbroken line of great souls who, without assuming for themselves, or in the name of God, or their being made to assume by enthusiastic followers, the attributes of a divine law-giver or God on earth and what-not, have been there to guide honest seekers who desire lasting peace and happiness and perfect understanding.

To those who may object that such a teacher is also a case of the truth being posited outside one's self, I would answer that it is so at first, but as I have already stated, his special function is to show his disciples the truth within themselves. The question may also be raised as to whether there is a difference between a spiritual teacher with a few disciples and the founder of a religion. Now granting for argument's sake that the founder of a religion has attained perfection, which is not necessarily the case, there can be absolutely no difference between him and a fully realized teacher, since both are essentially beyond distinctions. The distinction is one of appearances only, one with which we are not in the least concerned. As I said, a true spiritual teacher is not a man at all. He has identified himself with the reality, and being himself beyond body and mind, that is to say, beyond individuality, he sees none in others, indeed, he sees no others, but sees the self, pure consciousness, alone. How then, it may well be asked, can he teach others, when he sees none? The answer of course is that it is the others who think they are being taught by a teacher.

But, however much we may try to understand such a being, we shall not succeed. The idea I have attempted to convey of a spiritual teacher applies with equal force to one who, though beyond limitation, has no disciples. We can think about the truth and see that it is nothing but being, consciousness and bliss, but just as we cannot attain it by reason alone, we cannot understand the nature of a spiritual teacher. When we rise to that level where all that is unreal vanishes because the reality alone shines, we shall become one in that which seemed at first to be endowed with a body and mind. According to a man's sincerity so will he find a true teacher. And having found him, he will find that his heart's desire to know the truth becomes crystallized in what at first appears as a deep personal attachment to his teacher, who is seen as the embodiment of wisdom and love. This love directed towards the person of the teacher is really directed towards the impersonal reality. The disciple expresses his doubts and difficulties and the teacher by his answers removes them. As the disciple rises from level to level, so does this relationship deepen, until going beyond all personality, union is finally attained in the ultimate. I shall stop here, because this will be experienced by those fortunate enough to desire it: no words can describe it. I must add, for those who still see bodies and minds as such, that the union of the teacher and disciple is an inward and not an outward one. Furthermore, the word union is a misnomer for want of a better word because the oneness was always there but not recognized.

This aspect of spiritual guidance is quite unknown to the majority of mankind. To those who are familiar with it, the mere mention of a spiritual teacher may often bring tears to their eyes; but, whether it is the one or the other who seeks the truth, this is a fresh discovery that has to be made, the discovery of one's predestined master. Without him, however many books are read, and no matter what other learned man is consulted, the truth cannot be approached. It is the sincerity of the seeker that inevitably leads to the discovery of his teacher, and no one need despair. When the highest teacher is found, all the rest is assured.

V. THE PRESENT ETERNITY

My survey of the general principles of philosophy, its aim and its practice, was completed with the fourth talk. I concluded by speaking of the necessity of guidance in the form of a spiritual teacher that a seeker must have. And I showed that this is intimately connected with the seeker's sincerity. In my opening remarks to these talks, I said that the purpose of philosophy is to answer the questions that occur to every thinking man and woman, such questions as, "What am I?", and "What is the purpose of this existence?" and I went on to say that when the right answers are given *and* understood, such a revolution in the mind of the seeker is brought about that until he has experienced them in the most concrete manner, he feels he cannot rest.

It would be too much to expect that all those to whom this subject is new would have had such a strong feeling. This survey has covered a large area and the different points dealt with would require much discussion to relate their meaning to each man's personal experience. That is why a competent guide is needed, for he alone can immediately see where the obstacles to understanding lie in a particular man. What I can do here is only to state the truth and some hearts may be touched.

Those on the other hand who are familiar with the subject may have been able to follow the arguments that I have used. I spoke just now of the answers having not only to be understood but felt. This feeling is the essential here: many people are content to rest with the mental agreement, but I wish to emphasize that this cannot in any way give a real understanding, because as it has been made clear on many occasions, that which is beyond the mind is equally beyond the mind's grasp. Reason serves to overcome our mental obstacles, but the truth has to be experienced in the depth of our being: this experience of the truth, which is our real self, can be had only in the presence of one who has himself realized it, provided of course that we ourselves desire this experience above all, that is to say, provided we are quite sincere and earnest.

Why have I said these words? Whosoever has been able to grasp the contents of the previous talks will know in his heart if those words are necessary or not. And to those who have found it difficult to follow on account of the unfamiliarity of the subject-matter, I wish to give encouragement by the knowledge that although the answers given are in themselves self-evident, otherwise they were not true, the long habit of taking for granted the world as it appears and ourselves as we appear is a barrier that often stands in the way of mental agreement, though even before it has been got rid of, the truth can be directly experienced when it is heard from one who knows what he says. This habit is a false one as I have shown; the whole purpose of these talks is the practical one of showing its falsity and what the correct attitude is. In these two final talks, I propose to go over the whole ground again, enlarging on this point or that, adding further and higher conclusions where it seems useful to do so and confirming, I hope, in those who have been interested the desire to continue in the pursuit of true knowledge and lasting happiness until nothing more remains to be done and perfection is attained.

The cause of all our troubles and the obstacles to our finding lasting happiness is our wrongly associating the changeless principle we refer to as "I" with a body and a mind. This changeless principle may be viewed, in relation to man as he appears, either as the real self, or as absolute existence, consciousness, and bliss. We call it the real self as contrasted with the individual person, and I proved that what we refer to in ourselves as "I myself" is really nothing but a thought, just one among others. Before we even begin to speak or act, we are ready to come out with such a thought as "I did", "I saw" or "I thought"; but we know now that we are never the doer, perceiver or enjoyer, but the witness of our mental and bodily functions, since we are able to remember them afterwards. The mind is always changing, and unless there were some permanent background upon which a record of past events were made, it would be impossible to recall them. This argument admirably proves the presence of a changeless background that undoubtedly exists within us and that is all it is intended to do. Here memory is taken for granted, because it is something we all experience, but we should take nothing for granted and I am therefore going to look into the nature of memory. Now there is an obvious inconsistency in the two statements that the real self we refer to as "I" is not the doer, perceiver, or enjoyer and that this same changeless principle witnesses the actions of the mind and body. Witnessing is an act, and an act is a change. The idea of memory rests entirely upon the assumption that there is a witness to our actions: can this witnessing function belong to the mind? In one of these talks, I showed that the mind cannot be at two things at once, in other words there is only one thought at a time. I had already reduced the outer world into thought, so when I say that there can only be one thought at a time, it must be taken as including actions of the body and sense-perceptions. If we were able to have two or more thoughts at a time, we should need two or more individualities to claim them, otherwise one of the thoughts would be lost, and we could never know we had had it. Or we may say that the fact that we remember thoughts successively and not simultaneously is the adequate proof that there cannot be more than one thought at a time. Anyway, if memory were a function of the mind, the witnessing function or thought would be present along with the thought that is being witnessed, that is to say, there would be two concurrent thoughts and that, as we have seen, is impossible. Moreover it is not according to our experience that memory is present along with other thoughts any more than is the I-thought, which comes up just before and immediately after, but not during an act. When we are actually feeling thirst, there is the feeling alone and not the thought connecting it with ourselves; when we are thinking, "I am feeling thirsty", we are not at that moment aware of the feeling of thirst. Memory with its contents is therefore a thought among others exactly like the I-thought. It cannot be a function of pure consciousness, which is there whether there is thought or not, because pure consciousness has no function. There is nothing outside it upon which it can act, because nothing exists except in consciousness; memory also appears in consciousness. Thus memory is nothing but a thought, and it is closely connected with that function of the mind that claims for the individual all the acts done by the body and the mind, and at the same time, it is inseparable from consciousness. What does all this lead to?

Let us cast our minds back to what I said about time in the second of these talks. I am going to refer back to this question since memory obviously brings in the time element and what I said about it then will help us to arrive at the answer we are now seeking. What I said was: "Is not time the name we give to the intangible and indefinite something in which our thoughts occur? We measure time by fixed periods or intervals which we think of as past, present, or future. But the present is always past when we think of it and that is why I called time intangible". I shall interrupt this quotation to call attention to this fact that the present is always past when we think of it: is it not the same thing as what I said about the I-thought? When we say, "I see an elephant," we are not then seeing it although we use the present tense. If someone asks, "What are you doing?" we have to tell them what we *were* doing because hearing and answering his questions are new acts done since then. To continue the quotation with the last sentence: "But the present is already past when we think of it and that is I called time intangible. That which is always present is consciousness, whether we think of past or future. It is impossible to think of time without thinking of succession," and I now add, "it is equally impossible to think of memory without thinking of succession". And to proceed: "Nor can we think of succession without referring to time," and I again add, "nor can we think of succession without referring to memory". To continue: "But the actual thought appears *now* in consciousness," and it could equally well have been said, "the actual rememberance appears *now* in consciousness". To quote again, "That consciousness is eternal because it is ever-present. It is present when there is thought, it is present when there is no thought. If not, how could we speak of there being no thought? We become aware of time when we think of it: if we don't think of it, we are not aware of it. But we never cease to be aware or conscious, for consciousness never sleeps. Thus thoughts and time are one, one in consciousness". I have given the whole passage because it leads by steps to the last statement, that thoughts and time are one in consciousness. But memory is also a thought, so we may say that memory and time are one. Now we have just seen that the thought of past, present, and future is always *now*. We don't go back into yesterday to think of yesterday, nor do we travel forward into next week to make our next week's appointments. We do it at present and we are always in the present. What we remember is previous thoughts, that is to say, we have a thought now that concerns the past or the future. But can we say that a past thought exists unless we now think of it? We have seen that the kind of thought we call remembrance is not with other thoughts when they occur; nor were they witnessed by consciousness, so what proof have we that we ever had a previous thought, or that we shall ever have one in the future? We can only think of it now in any case. There is indeed absolutely no proof that other thoughts exist. There is in consequence no proof whatsoever that there is a past or a future or what we try to catch hold of and call the present. What alone exists is consciousness: time or memory is quite illusory. If there is any thought at all, there is one only; and if only one, it is no longer a thought. The deep understanding that memory is simply a thought takes us at once out of time into pure consciousness. Between the thinker and the thought there is the thinking or pure experience. I had previously described experience as a moment of consciousness in order to help comprehension, and similarly in the present context, I shall now describe the indescribable consciousnesss as the present eternity. It is this that shines in every experience. It also shines when there is no outward experience and this brings us to a further consideration of deep sleep.

I have spoken of deep sleep on several occasions: in deep sleep, although the mind and the body are both absent, we retain our essential consciousness and it is this that enables us to say on waking, "I enjoyed sound sleep" or "I knew nothing." It is this so-called nothing that I am now going to examine. We have already seen that this nothing or no thing is in contrast with what we perceive when we are awake or dreaming. Now I ask this question: Is it possible to know nothing? By nothing, we refer to something absent, absent either to our senses or to our mind. Anything that is so absent can certainly not be known or perceived. And what is ignorance? Ignorance is also posited with reference to what is not present to our consciousness. Can we say that something not present to our consciousness exists? If so, we know it, otherwise we could not say that it exists. Consequently, there is no such thing as ignorance and when we say that in deep sleep we know nothing, we are making a mistake. We can know only what is present and in deep sleep, what is present is consciousness and peace, our real nature. We cannot know it as an object because it is our own self, so the verb to know would be wrongly used here. All we can say, and it is correct, is that in deep sleep, we subsist as our real self in the absolute state. Though the false limitation to a body and a mind, or of space and time, is absent, the realization of this perfection is prevented by our attitude before and after sleep. We talk of sleeping away the world and of knowing nothing and this is what spoils the experience. If we take to the thought that in the absence of objective experience, consciousness remains, the so-called ignorance of deep sleep will in time give way to the light of consciousness shining in its own glory.

This experience is not confined to deep sleep. I have already referred to absent-mindedness and the same thing applies to what is between thoughts. I am now speaking from a level where the succession of thoughts and memory as such are accepted. Any talk on spiritual matters has to be conducted on different planes at different times so as to comprise the great variety of our worldly experience. Contradictions may appear on the surface, but as all this has for its purpose the attainment of that in which all contradictions vanish we need only see from what level we are talking for the difficulty to disappear. It must never be forgotten that there are always contradictions between different planes. Even now, starting from where the existence of thoughts and memory as such is admitted, we shall find ourselves in a few minutes at the place in which consciousness shines by itself.

Before and after every thought, feeling, or perception, there is an interval, just as in the movement of a pendulum at the end of each swing, there is a moment of rest. Without such an interval, there would be one continuous thought, but that is not what we find. In this interval, we are neither dead nor asleep nor have we any consciousness of our bodies and minds.

Where are we then? If we say that we were without any thought, it is not incorrect but it is negative. What was present was consciousness or our real self, just as in deep sleep. So here again, we have to be thinking that between two thoughts, it is not nothing, but awareness and peace that remain. To make this point quite clear, let us take as an example a glass of water. If the water is thrown away and we ask someone what is in the glass, he will say that nothing is in it. He is not stating exactly what he sees, but he is making a comparison between what was previously seen and what is seen now. What he unknowingly says is that the consciousness which revealed the full glass reveals also the empty one. And this is what we mean when we say that between two thoughts, there are no thoughts, instead of saying that there was consciousness. Because we only recognize consciousness when it is related to the body or the mind, we make these the standard whereas the true standard is consciousness itself. What we have to do therefore is to rid ourselves of the habit of thinking of nothing or of ignorance or of absence and indeed, of anything negative, since no such thing exists. Here again, I am not suggesting that we should expunge all negative words from our vocabulary; we need them in ordinary life. All we have to do is to make sure we know what we are talking about and then the use of such words will not tie us down. If we always keep before us the idea of consciousness being present whether the mind is active or at rest, we shall gradually become centred in it and going beyond all questions of being and not being, find peace.

We have just seen how we tend to refer one thing back to another; this was in connection with the state of pure consciousness experienced in deep sleep and between two thoughts, instead of seeing it as the positive state it is, we describe it negatively in terms of what was there before. The same tendency is also to be found in what we posit as the chain of cause and effect. This brings us to a very important point. When speaking of the perceiver and the perceived or the subject and the object, I stated that both terms are complementary. Speaking from a higher level, when considering the nature of the I-thought, I showed that at the time of an object's being perceived, there is no notion of the perceiver: when the thought of the perceiver comes in, the object of perception has vanished from our mind. In other words, the perceiver and the perceived, or the subject and the object, never exist together. If there is an object and no perceiver, it is wrong to call it an object of perception. If there is the perceiver but nothing perceived, the word perceiver is not applicable. The idea of a perceiver and an object of perception is conceived only when the mind claims the action afterwards in the name of I-myself. It is, as we have seen, just a thought or rather a collection of several thoughts, including those of the individual, the knower, the known, and the knowledge, and it is most misleading because there is in fact no such thing as a subject or an object. As I have shown, there is the middle term common to both, that of perceiving, doing or enjoying, and this is pure experience connected with something objective; as that something is also nothing other than consciousness, there is pure experience alone. The whole world then becomes transformed into what it really is, namely, absolute consciousness.

Now what I have been saying will help us in our analysis of cause and effect. Cause and effect are like the subject and the object; just as an object is related to a subject, so is an effect the result of a cause. Sometimes we draw directly upon memory to connect cause with effect; at other times, we gratuitously posit a cause. For instance, we see a tree for the first time and think of it as being twelve years old; all our worldly habits of thought support such an idea but reason is quite against it. We have already seen that memory is simply a thought and so it cannot be brought forward as a proof. And in the example of the tree, we are assuming that in spite of changes which in any case we have not witnessed, it is the same one that existed twelve years ago. But in fact, the notion of "twelve-years-old" is a single, present thought we have now. In all these talks, I have taken change for granted in order to point out from the level where we started that behind all apparent change, there is a changeless principle. I shall conclude this talk by proving that nothing changes and in the meantime, I have to show that there is no such thing as cause and effect.

When something is said to be the effect of a cause, we may reasonably expect to find two separate entities, the cause and the effect. But two such corresponding entities are never found to exist at once. For example, when we look for a cause, we lose sight of the effect:

this is because when whatever it is we afterwards call the cause existed, the effect had not come into being. If we look at something we think of as being an effect, we see that thing only and not the cause: that is because when something has taken effect, the cause has ceased to exist. To take the old example of a large tree growing out of a small seed, the seed contains within it, we say, the germ or the cause not only of one tree but of endless generations of trees. But suppose the seed had failed to germinate, or had fallen on a rock, or water was lacking or in excess during that time, or that a bird had eaten the seed. Can the seed alone have been the cause, even though it did in fact send out shoots and become in time a fully grown tree? No particular effect can possibly have been observed in the seed, it might as well have become something else, for instance, food for a bird or a medicine, according to its kind. If the gradual change in the seed from the time of its falling off the tree until it began to send out shoots were brought forward as an argument to show the signs of effect in the seed, I would answer that in each stage of its development the seed is no longer the same as what it was before: something entirely new is seen each time and not the original thing as it was with an effect added. If we look at the fully grown tree, however much we may look for the original seed, we shall never find it, just as the milk and the churning are lost irrevocably when the butter has formed. In other words, the cause passes over into the effect and in the absence of cause, where is effect? And without effect, where is cause? Now this is not a playing with words as a superficial person would be tempted to think; on the contrary, it gives words their proper meaning. When the world as such is taken for granted, there is certainly cause and effect, but we are taking nothing for granted, not even the current usage of words. We have been able to understand that a thing exists when and because we perceive it and not otherwise. The ideas of cause and effect, like and dislike and the claiming I-thought are all dependent upon memory and memory alone. But we know that memory has no real existence; it is a thought, and if memory is the basis of cause and effect, cause and effect are meaningless words. Thus subject and object, cause and effect, and all other like conceptions are themselves a play upon words: they fall to pieces on examination.

As for change, we think of it also in virtue of memory. We lend permanency to fleeting perceptions because instead of seeing the permanency where it really is, that is, in ourselves, we attribute it to things outside ourselves. If a thing changes, it becomes something new and there is nothing left by which we can connect it with a previous thing, unless it is memory. The identity of a measure of milk cannot be the same as that of the lump of butter we say it becomes. How therefore can the milk be said to have changed into butter? We have seen that effect is never seen in cause nor cause in effect. The world is at every new perception a new world. As I said in the second of these talks, the universe rises and subsides in consciousness. It has no existence apart from ourselves. There is no change, no cause and no effect, no perceiver and no perceived, no comparison between this and that, no ignorance or limitation and therefore no knowledge or freedom; all contraries meet in what we have come to see as the only reality, in consciousness, in the self.

VI. Freedom

The ideas of knower and known, cause and effect, comparison of this with that, and change are all dependent upon one thing and one thing alone, and that is memory. In the last talk, I showed that memory has no substance: it is a simple thought like any other, and even though it contains the idea of past time, thought of past is always now. Projecting the principle of memory into the future, it becomes a hope or a plan and there also we saw that thought of future is now. We saw that when memory is known as thought, the idea of time at once goes: time is known by the succession of thoughts and this is based upon memory. Since memory is a thought and nothing more, there is no proof that other thoughts exist, because we can only have one thought at a time. Other thoughts exist when we think of them; we think of them always now. That means that if there is thought at all, there can be one only, and that is certainly no ordinary thought. What really exists is consciousness and in this particular context of time and memory, I described it as the present eternity. Of course the truth can never be described: but it can be pointed to by indications and that is what I have been doing in all these talks.

Now I have just made reference to the present eternity. When I was speaking of change at the end of my previous talk, I proved that at every perception, there is a new world. It is created when we think of it and it is destroyed when thought is absent. The universe rises and subsides in consciousness which is our real self. We must never forget that our body and mind are also a part of the universe and that it is through this part that we know it. Although I say they are parts of it, our bodies and minds are themselves the universe, because by the mind's going out through the physical and subtle organs of sense, the universe is born. In every perception, there is the perceiving, a moment of pure consciousness or experience, and therefore the world cannot be separated from consciousness without which it has no existence whatsoever. To speak of a moment of consciousness may give rise to the wrong impression that apart from that moment, consciousness lapses. I use the word moment not in reference to time but to convey the idea that awareness is the kernel of every experience. There is no experience, whether in the form of a thought, feeling, or perception, or without form as in deep sleep or between two thoughts, that is not of the nature of consciousness. And here I have to dispel a conception that I have not yet questioned; it no longer serves any purpose and even stands as an obstacle to our further progress. It is the idea that there is difference between a state in which thoughts occur and one in which consciousness shines alone, to use the expression which has now run its course. It is from the mind level that we talk of thoughts or their absence. We have seen that consciousness is always present; it is beyond name and form and thus from its own level, it alone exists. I add that it is beyond states or levels which belong to the mind. I spoke of it as the one of the many: it would have been truer to speak of the many of the one, to give the right order. Ultimately there is neither one nor many. Whatever we say about it is only a pointer and nothing more, but if by this attempt a chord within us is struck, its purpose is fulfilled.

However extraordinary it may sound, I cannot refrain from interrupting this talk to speak of happiness because any talk of the absolute has the immediate effect of giving one a taste of absolute bliss which is one with consciousness. As we have seen, when the mind is focused upon any thing, it becomes that thing. If we look at a table or think of a flower, the mind then becomes the table or the flower. When it is directed towards consciousness, its source, it merges in consciousness and that is the same as happiness or love. A deep understanding of the truth is accompanied always by this feeling of happiness that rises with it. Let this feeling be the measure of our understanding. If the understanding is complete, so is our felicity.

When we know someone well, we cannot help loving him. It is impossible to know someone well unless the knower's personality is kept aside. When our personality, or in other words, our mind, is not in the way, we are beyond the mind; we are at one with our self. This is absolute existence, consciousness and love or happiness: no wonder that we feel love then. There is this also, that mind through bodies knows bodies, mind in itself knows mind, and the self, beyond body and mind, is at one with the self, as we have just seen. We can now talk of loving our neighbour as our self. Our neighbour is not our neighbour when we perceive him. When we afterwards think of him as being our neighbour, that thought is also an experience in the self. And even hatred is only pure love, conditioned by the forethought or the afterthought of something that concerns bodies or minds. This again shows the consequence of blindly accepting memory. When memory is known for what it is, we can only love. And that is not love for someone, that is to say, for some object of perception, since there is no such thing: it is self-love. I am not advocating some insipid sentimental path; sentiment is love tied up in memory. I am simply showing where the reality lies; if we seek the real and see through the illusory, we establish ourselves in peace, regardless of seeming appearances.

I said just now that mind through bodies knows bodies and mind in itself knows mind. In all these talks, the body and mind have been treated as quite distinct in order to show how the reality runs through our everyday experience. It was because of this that in proving the real nature of the principle we refer to as I-myself, the sense-organs were taken as belonging to the body. I stated that the body as such is inert. But since the organs of sense function always as the instruments of consciousness, they cannot properly be called inert, although they are also of flesh. And in examining the mind, it was seen that it functions always in terms of the senses which in the mind appear as the subtle sense-organs. Once, however, it is understood that the mind can never stand apart from the body, inasmuch as the sense-perceptions, even when subtle, refer in every case to something material, the difference, if any, between body and mind, or the gross and the subtle, is no more than one of degree, and then only when the emphasis is on the body. It is in terms of the body that we speak of an outer world while the world of thought appears as an inner one. What is it from the standpoint of the mind? Obviously, for the mind there is neither an inner nor an outer world but only thought. We have already seen that the world exists only when we think of it. It follows that the body and the so-called material universe are simply thoughts, without any question of degree. In every thought of the world, the sense-organs are implicit. For example, if we think of someone, we see him with what we call the mind's eye. If we think of a tune, the sense of hearing comes in. And even abstract thoughts have an object so that there also, the senses are implied. But no thought is possible without the presence of consciousness. Thus on the one hand, there is consciousness, and on the other there are the organs of sense, standing for body and mind. Now a sensation is a conscious perception, and as it is on account of the different kinds of sensation that we posit the different organs of sense, we need consider sensations only and they too are of the nature of consciousness from which they are inseparable. All is therefore that consciousness.

Why there is consciousness alone and why consciousness alone is real can now be proved in a more direct manner than has been possible hitherto. If we wish to know something, that something assumes for the time being the quality appropriate to the sense-organ through which it is apprehended, that is to say, if we direct our attention to it through the eyes, it is known as a form and if we do so through the ears, it is known as a sound. Though a form or a sound is perceived, the thing in itself is unknown. In the absence of sight or hearing, there is no form or sound, but something is there nevertheless. If we give it a name, that too is not the thing as it really is; to name a thing is simply to associate it with other things about which we are no wiser. What is called knowing a thing consists in giving it name and form, but neither of these is the thing itself. I hit still, something is there. What is it? Something that exists without name and form, what can it be but existence itself? And does not existence always shine? By this, what I mean is that in some way or another, existence makes itself known, and that means it is one with consciousness. In relation to life, it is called absolute existence, in relation to thought, pure consciousness, and in relation to feeling, pure love or happiness. But since beyond the mind there are no distinctions, these three are one. Therefore things, whether perceived or felt, as they really are and we ourselves as we are really, are one and the same. We think we know this or that object by such and such a quality when in fact we cannot know anything at all with the senses, because it is to these, and not to the so-called objects, that the so-called qualities belong. This then is the truth about it, that all is one consciousness, one reality.

Let us return now to the question of there being something or nothing which arises from the consideration of thoughts and their absence. There is in truth neither something nor nothing ! Something is present, nothing is absent. Now I have proved that awareness is ever-present; when something is spoken of as being present, reference is made to the possibility of absence. It is our experience that consciousness, the changeless principle we refer to as "I", is never absent and so such a suggestion has no place here. And whatever is thought of as present refers really to the presence of consciousness. There is, therefore neither something nor nothing. Many of the terms used to denote the ultimate reality are either negative in form or one of a pair of opposites. This is evidently because any positive word refers to something within the grasp of the mind, so we call it absolute existence, knowledge or bliss, transcendental, non-dual or changeless to show that it is beyond the mind. It may help us to speak of absolute existence, though that suggests the possibility of there being a relative existence, a false suggestion. If we call it absolute consciousness, it assumes that there is a limited one, a wrong assumption. If we call it absolute happiness or love, it presumes there may be impure happiness or love, a gross presumption. By calling it self-luminous, it may also help us, because granting the existence of relative things, these require the light of consciousness to illuminate them, whereas awareness is self-illuminating. This is why we speak of absolute existence; unlike individual life, which we think of as needing a higher principle to quicken it, pure being is self-subsisting and so also are absolute consciousness and bliss. But by constantly directing the mind to what lies beyond it on the basis of everyday experience as pointed out by one who knows it, the mind subsides not in the ignorance of sleep but in the light of reality.

I spoke right at the beginning of the waking, dream and deep-sleep states in order to prove the existence of a changeless background of consciousness, the principle we refer to as "I" when talking of ourselves. Speaking of dreams, I observe that there is no proof that we are not dreaming even now. In the dream state, what we experience never appears to us as a dream: on the contrary, it is as concrete as what we now experience in the waking state. It is only when we wake that we think of it as having been a dream. We also think of it as unreal. Let us compare the two states and see whether any difference can be found. In both states, we ourselves appear as the doer, perceiver and enjoyer; in both states, there are the actions done, the things perceived and enjoyed or suffered, the people we meet and the use of reason. They are both exactly the same. In a dream, as I have said, our experiences there seem no less concrete than those we have when we are awake. A distinction is made nevertheless, by our calling a dream unreal when it is remembered on waking. We know already what memory is, and we know that the dream rises in our mind as a simple thought; we have it in the present, but that is not the argument I am now using. The point I am making is that if a dream is unreal as it undoubtedly is when viewed from the waking state, is not the waking state also quite unreal, since when both states are looked at without prejudice, there is no means of differentiating them? No proof can be given to establish the reality of the waking state when none exists to prove that of the dream state. It might be argued that we do all the same experience the world of the waking state as real, and that being so, the dream state must also be real, since both are equal. There is no doubt that this would be in order if the reality of our waking experiences could be established. But we have seen over and over again that it cannot, because our perceptions in themselves are non-existent while consciousness alone is existent. So it matters not whether we think of this or that relative thing or state as real or unreal since the thought itself is illogical. Accepting however for the moment the distinction between real and unreal, we are bound to admit that since the waking state which is based upon body consciousness has no existence apart from pure consciousness, it is in itself quite unreal. If it is unreal, it can have no more existence than the dream state. We saw a short while ago that the ultimate reality is beyond all states and this proves it; we know it to be always present, even in the two non-existent states we have just disposed of. We have only to follow the unconditioned for the so-called conditioned to vanish together with the necessity of positing its opposite, the unconditioned reality, and all our problems are solved.

We hear much talk nowadays about freedom. But what freedom is there so long as we think we are limited by time and space or mind and body? Freedom lies within us, it is always there for the seeking, but we take everything for granted and so continue in bondage. We are bound to life and death because we believe in them. Believing we were born, we are sure to die, but birth and death are both changes. I have already proved that there is no such thing as a change. We have fresh perceptions and, bringing down the idea of the changeless to the level where perceptions may be said to occur, we attribute a common identity to quite different objects of perception and say that one thing has changed, but this is not possible. There is therefore no such thing as birth and death: both are changes. He is immortal who knows he was never born. He is happy who knows no ignorance. He is wise who is always at peace. To be at peace is not to oppose ignorance: that is ignorant. Peace is attained when it is known as one's self.

The Universal Religion

This essay on the Universal Religion is appended to these talks because, although written independently, it sums up the whole matter in a few lines besides making clear the position of the essential Hindu religion in its relation to others. It seems to me, therefore, that it makes a fitting conclusion.

This is about Hinduism, the universal religion. There are people who count the number of adherents to all religions and then make comparisons. There are others who see which religion has its followers amongst the greatest number of the nations and draw conclusions. But I would ask you to consider which religion embraces the widest variety of human types. The larger the number of human types, the larger the number of ways, ways to the goal of religion, and the more universal that religion.

For every individual, the goal is different, not in itself, but as it appears when seen from without. While some consciously seek it, others are indifferent. To the first category, direct guidance must be available to help them in their search by bringing the truth nearer and nearer until it is realized as one's self. To the second, means must be given to keep them within certain safe limits and the possibility always left open for a direct approach to the truth. This is at a social rather than at a purely spiritual level; by drawing attention to family duties and social obligations, the egoism of the individual is slowly reduced until room is made for some light from above to enter, and he will then begin to seek it consciously.

Allowance must be made for the differences in nature between one man and another; the causes of these must also be considered. These causes come down from previous lives and this explains the more or less advanced state of human development in each man and his various tendencies. These tendencies have to be worked out and because at present what is known as the Hindu religion exists only in one place on earth, people may be born in other places as members of other religions in circumstances other than those to be found in India.

When looked at from this aspect, it is clear that there is only one religion whatever name it gets. It is noticeable throughout the world that the higher a man rises spiritually, the more he approaches the corresponding degree in the basic religion, basic because it is at once the most ancient, the most constant and the most generally expressive of all, but chiefly because it is the highest.

If a man goes quite beyond limitation, he goes beyond degrees and therefore beyond religion itself. The Hindu conceptions of doctrine and practice alone can take him there. How is that? Is it not because it is always understood that religion is not an end but a means? Other religions cling to their practice or else to their ideas, but the two never seem to rise together as one, accompanying the seeker until they serve no more purpose. They are often in conflict. How so? Because other religions depend in part or wholly upon the teachings of a master given centuries ago to suit people of some other time and place whereas this religion has an unbroken line of masters, each perfect, who can express the truth and prescribe practices to suit each single individual according to his need. The past is always respected and always followed, but not so as to cover up the present. The truth is known to be ever-present and therefore the Hindu religion is evergreen. It might be objected that in no other religion is there so much that is base and obsolete. If it is so, I would not object: it embraces every possibility.

But there is no other religion that is so elevated. The essential Hindu religion is known as Vedanta (Advaita) or the end of knowledge. All the rest is at most a preparation; it cannot be compared with other religions however since it has Vedanta in its midst as its flower. It may be said to be nearer the centre no matter at what level it is viewed, on the analogy of a spiral staircase whose inner rise is nearer to the axis than its outer one. It is in the nature of things that in the land where it is found, the whole range of human development from the lowest to the very highest should be seen. The aim is to go beyond all that is relative and when all is truly seen as relative, and one's own personality is known to be a part of that relativity, the absolute is attained.

That is why the essential Hinduism centres around the real self in man, that which is changeless, and is not based on the relationship between man and God. The reality in man is what he refers to as I-myself and the thing which prevents his knowing it as such is the habit of identifying it with the body and the mind. To sever this false association is all that is needed for him to attain the perfection he always was. What other religion offers so simple and so self-evident a path as this? Anyone, at any time and at any place can understand it, no matter what temperament he may possess. It cuts through all suffocating ritual and the dusty books and traditions of ordinary religion; it breathes fresh air. The only requisite is earnestness and sincerity. In the true Hindu, sincerity is the true orthodoxy. Thus all sincere souls are Hindus, whatever they are called and wherever they may be. That is why I call Hinduism the universal religion. Or perhaps it would be better to call the universal religion Vedanta, since it is not limited to any place, as the word Hindu suggests.

October, 1946.

[1.] See the author's *The Nature of Man According to the Vedanta'* Ch. XXVIII, 2, on 'The Origin of Identification.'

Dedication

The universal Religion went into recess when Govinda Guru thrust out of his cave a single foot to be clasped by Sri Shankara and then withdrew it. From that time onward, renunciation of an unexplained world became the vogue, even though the other foot came out for a moment in the form of Vidyaranya. Now, with both feet firmly planted in a world of selfless action, it has come out into the open after a long and refreshing retreat. The owner of those two blessed limbs is the great Teacher Sri Atmananda whose outer name of Krishna gives the clue. There is no more need to put on ochre garments and to sit within a ring of fearful fire. White is now the colour and in it every shade is there. Let ropes be taken for snakes or snakes for ropes! Who cares who knows that whatever it is, the thing in itself is one's self! So the world is explained in a wonderful way, not pushed away, but allowed to stay as oneself, and that with no evasion. What is the self but the core of existence, the light in thought and the love in emotion, the one of the many, the many of the one, and I am the key to the puzzle. It is I who exist in and I who perceive and it is I who enjoy or complain of the things that are known by me or else they are absent: I am the life of their being. With this as one's sword, the world as it comes may be faced with courage, and thanks be paid to my glorious Teacher Sri Atmananda Guru, beneath whose feet I place this work.

About this book . . .

John Levy here attempts to answer the question which has always puzzled mankind: 'What am I?'

To achieve his aim the author enlists the aid of Hindu philosophy, specifically the essential Hindu doctrine of Vedanta, 'the end of knowledge,' and its highest aspect of Advaita, or Non-Duality. Vedanta maintains a perfect balance of theory and practice and is therefore capable of immediate application.

Our essential being is something other than the mind and the body we claim to possess. The author demonstrates that in fact we cannot identify with either. It is the body that is hungry, feels cold. It is the mind that thinks, remembers and desires. A case of simple possession is mistaken for identity with the thing possessed.

'When I say I own a house I don't imply that I am a house. On the contrary, I cannot possibly be one. The sense of possessing a house is in no way different from the sense of possessing a mind or a body. A body, like a house, is an object, and so is a mind. But I am the possessor of the object and therefore not the object itself, in this case the body or the mind. In other words, if I possess a body and a mind, I am clearly other than the body or the mind.'

If man is not the body and mind he believes himself to be, what is he? John Levy answers that in his real nature man is being, consciousness, and bliss. He must become centred in his true self and this is accomplished by his separating himself from the body idea. In the words of the 'Ashtavakra Samhita', quoted by the author, 'If you separate yourself from the body and rest in consciousness, you will at once be happy, peaceful and free from bondage.'

SENTIENT PUBLICATIONS, LLC
PO BOX 1851
BOULDER CO 80306
303-443-2188
contact@sentientpublications.com
www.sentientpublications.com

www.ingramcontent.com/pod-product-compliance
Lightning Source LLC
Chambersburg PA
CBHW011408070526
44586CB00021B/2581